# NORWAY

R.L. Van

**Big Buddy Books**
An Imprint of Abdo Publishing
abdobooks.com

# abdobooks.com

Published by Abdo Publishing, a division of ABDO, PO Box 398166, Minneapolis, Minnesota 55439.
Copyright © 2023 by Abdo Consulting Group, Inc. International copyrights reserved in all countries. No part of this book may be reproduced in any form without written permission from the publisher. Big Buddy Books™ is a trademark and logo of Abdo Publishing.

Printed in the United States of America, North Mankato, Minnesota
102022
012023

Design: Emily O'Malley, Mighty Media, Inc.
Production: Mighty Media, Inc.
Editor: Jessica Rusick
Cover Photograph: Olena Tur/Shutterstock Images
Interior Photographs: Damien VERRIE/Shutterstock Images, p. 6 (top); Dmitry Naumov/Shutterstock Images, p. 27 (bottom); fifg/Shutterstock Images, p. 29 (bottom right); Filip Bjorkman/Shutterstock Images, p. 7 (map); giedre vaitekune/Shutterstock Images, p. 26 (right); Globe Turner/Shutterstock Images, p. 30 (flag); Harvepino/Shutterstock Images, p. 13; JaHu83/Shutterstock Images, p. 30 (currency); LINGTREN.COM/Shutterstock Images, p. 23; lukulo/iStockphoto, pp. 5 (compass), 7 (compass); MARIE LOUISE SOMBY/Wikimedia Commons, p. 9; Marius Dobilas/Shutterstock Images, pp. 6 (middle), 17; Nanisimova/Shutterstock Images, p. 27 (top left); Natalia_Kompaniets/Shutterstock Images, p. 19; Olena Znak/Shutterstock Images, p. 27 (top right); Paul D Smith/Shutterstock Images, p. 11; Paulo Miguel Costa/Shutterstock Images, p. 28 (bottom); Pyty/Shutterstock Images, p. 5 (map); R7 Photo/Shutterstock Images, p. 15; saiko3p/Shutterstock Images, p. 6 (bottom); Sigsand03/Wikimedia Commons, p. 21; Tatiana Popova/Shutterstock Images, p. 26 (left); Wikimedia Commons, pp. 28 (top), 29 (top), 29 (bottom left); WillemA/Shutterstock Images, p. 25
Design Elements: Mighty Media, Inc.
Country population and area figures taken from the CIA World Factbook

Library of Congress Control Number: 2022940504

**Publisher's Cataloging-in-Publication Data**
Names: Van, R.L., author.
Title: Norway / by R.L. Van
Description: Minneapolis, Minnesota : Abdo Publishing, 2023 | Series: Countries | Includes online resources and index.
Identifiers: ISBN 9781532199707 (lib. bdg.) | ISBN 9781098274900 (ebook)
Subjects: LCSH: Norway--Juvenile literature. | Europe--Juvenile literature. | Scandinavia--Juvenile literature. | Nordic countries--Juvenile literature. | Geography--Juvenile literature.
Classification: DDC 948.1--dc23

# CONTENTS

# PASSPORT TO NORWAY

Norway is a country in northern Europe. It is part of the **Scandinavian Peninsula**. More than 5.5 million people live there.

### SAY IT

**Svalbard**
*SVAHL-bahr*

**Jan Mayen**
*YAHN MYE-en*

### DID YOU KNOW?

Svalbard and Jan Mayen are island **territories** of Norway.

NORWAY

Atlantic Ocean

Sweden

Finland

Russia

North Sea

Baltic Sea

# IMPORTANT CITIES

Oslo is Norway's **capital** and largest city. It is a center for business, transportation, and the arts.

Bergen is Norway's second-largest city. It is surrounded by mountains. It is known for its education, history, and food.

Trondheim is Norway's third-largest city. It is known for its history, food, and culture.

**NORWAY**

**Trondheim**
Population: 210,496

**Bergen**
Population: 286,930

**Oslo**
Population: 1.07 million

**SAY IT**

**Oslo**
*AHZ-loh*

**Bergen**
*BUHR-gehn*

**Trondheim**
*TRAHN-haym*

# NORWAY IN HISTORY

People have lived in Norway for more than 10,000 years. One of the earliest groups was the Sami.

From about 800 to 1050, Vikings lived in Norway. They sailed to other lands and explored them.

## SAY IT

**Sami**
*SAH-mee*

Norway has a Sami Parliament. This political group serves the Sami people.

Norway joined with Sweden in 1319. From 1387 to 1814, Denmark controlled Norway. In 1814, Norway agreed to be ruled by Sweden's king. But it kept its own government. Norway became independent in 1905. Today, Norway is strong. Its government makes sure all people are cared for.

Norway celebrates its independence every May 17 on Constitution Day.

# AN IMPORTANT SYMBOL

Norway's flag has a dark blue Nordic cross. It is outlined in white on a red background.

Norway is a **parliamentary constitutional monarchy**. A group called the Storting makes laws. The prime minister is head of government. The king or queen is head of state.

The Nordic cross on Norway's flag represents Christianity.

# ACROSS THE LAND

● ● ● ● ● ● ● ● ● ● ● ● ●

Norway has **fjords**, rocky coasts, plains, mountains, and forests. It is home to the Lofoten Islands.

Norway has reindeer, elk, foxes, and birds. Salmon, whales, and seals live in its waters. Berries, moss, and many types of trees grow there.

**SAY IT**

fjord
*FYORD*

The Lofoten Islands are home to many small fishing villages.

# EARNING A LIVING

Many Norwegians have service jobs. They may work in education or government. Factory workers make ships and metal products.

Norway's **natural resources** include oil, natural gas, lumber, and fish. Farmers produce meat, milk, grains, and potatoes.

Norway is the fifth-largest exporter of oil in the world.

# LIFE IN NORWAY

Norway is known for its high standard of living. Popular foods include fish, lefse, cheese, and meats. Skiing, ice skating, hiking, and sailing are popular activities. Norwegians value traditions and enjoy folk tales and festivals. Many Norwegians are **Lutheran**.

Lefse is a flatbread made with potatoes. It is cooked on a griddle.

# FAMOUS FACES

Henrik Ibsen was born in Skien, Norway, in 1828. He studied to be a pharmacist but instead began writing plays. Ibsen became a successful **playwright**. He is known for his bold, sad stories. Ibsen died in 1906. Today, his plays are among the most-performed in the world.

Henrik Ibsen's works include *Brand*, *Peer Gynt*, and *A Doll's House*.

Magnus Carlsen grew up in Haslum, Norway. When he was five years old, his father taught him to play chess. In 2004, Carlsen became the youngest Grandmaster at the time at age 13. He became World Chess Champion in 2013. Carlsen continues to compete today.

Magnus Carlsen won the World Chess Championship five times.

23

# A GREAT COUNTRY

Norway has beautiful land and a rich history and culture. The people and places of Norway help make the world a more interesting place.

**····DID YOU····
KNOW?**

Norway has won more medals at the Winter Olympics than any other country.

Galdhøpiggen is the tallest mountain in Norway. It is a popular spot for hiking and skiing.

# TOUR BOOK

If you ever visit Norway, here are some places to go and things to do!

## HIKE

Hike to the top of Pulpit Rock. It is 1,982 feet (604 m) high!

## PLAY

Swim and slide at Bø Sommarland, Scandinavia's largest water park.

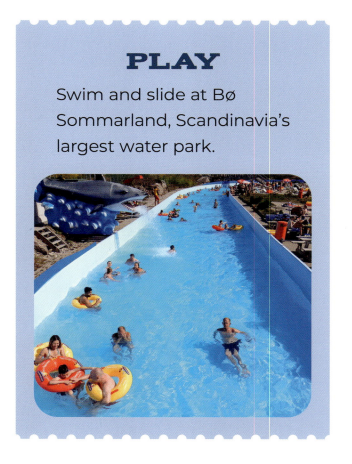

## DISCOVER

See more than 200 sculptures by Norwegian artist Gustav Vigeland at Vigeland Sculpture Park in Oslo.

## EXPLORE

Take a boat cruise to see Sognefjord. It is Norway's longest and deepest **fjord**.

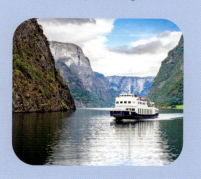

## LEARN

Find out more about Norway's history at the open-air Norwegian Folk Museum in Oslo.

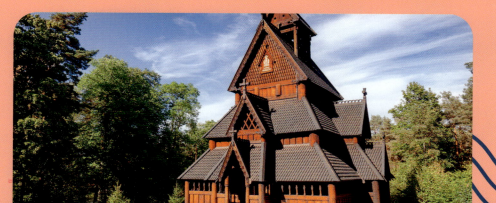

# TIMELINE

## AROUND 900

Harald I (*right*) became Norway's first king.

### 1299

Akershus Castle was built in Oslo. It is still used today.

### 1825

Sondre Norheim was born in southern Norway. He came up with new ski bindings that changed the sport of skiing. These allowed skiers to have more control and do more turns.

## 1981

Gro Harlem Brundtland became Norway's first female prime minister.

## 2011

**Terrorist** attacks in Oslo and on a nearby island killed 77 people.

## 1928

Norwegian figure skater Sonja Henie won her first Olympic gold medal. She won more Olympic and World medals than any other female figure skater.

## 2022

Norway earned 16 gold medals at the Winter Olympics in Beijing, the most the country had ever received at one Olympics.

# NORWAY UP CLOSE

**Official Name**
Kongeriket Norge
(Kingdom of Norway)

**Flag**

**Population**
5,553,840 (2022 est.)
117th-most-populated country

**Total Area**
125,021 square miles
(323,802 sq km)
68th-largest country

**Official Languages**
Norwegian, Sami

**Capital**
Oslo

**Currency**
Norwegian kroner

**Form of Government**
Parliamentary
constitutional
monarchy

**National Anthem**
"Ja, vi elsker dette
landet" ("Yes, We
Love This Country")

# GLOSSARY

**capital**—a city where government leaders meet.

**fjord**—a narrow section of ocean reaching into the land between two high cliffs.

**Lutheran**—a Christian who follows the teachings of Martin Luther.

**natural resources**—useful and valuable supplies from nature.

**parliamentary constitutional monarchy**—a form of government in which a parliament makes the laws. The king or queen has only those powers given by a country's laws and constitution.

**peninsula**—a stretch of land coming out from a mainland and almost entirely surrounded by water.

**playwright**—a person who writes plays.

**Scandinavian** (skan-duh-NAY-vee-uhn)—of or relating to the people, languages, or life in Sweden, Denmark, and Norway.

**territory**—an area that is not a state but is under the authority of a country's government.

**terrorist**—a person who uses violence to scare or control people or governments.

# ONLINE RESOURCES

To learn more about Norway, please visit **abdobooklinks.com** or scan this QR code. These links are routinely monitored and updated to provide the most current information available.

# INDEX